Blood Sonnets

poems by

Elizabeth L. Hodges

Finishing Line Press
Georgetown, Kentucky

Blood Sonnets

ACKNOWLEDGMENTS

"Jane Doe," *Matrix*
"Marie Antoinette," "Lucy," *113howl.com*
"Morgan Le Fey," "Guinevere," *Interim*
"Elizabeth I," "Rosa Parks," "Sophie Scholl," "Mary Shelley," *Taint, Taint, Taint*
"Lillian Hellman," *Ploughshares*
"Athena," "AKOLOUTE (Sequi me)," *Common*

Publisher: Leah Huete de Maines
Editor: Christen Kincaid
Cover Art: Nur, Havana, Cuba
Author Photo: Anna Halberstadt, New York City
Cover Design: Elizabeth Maines McCleavy

Order online: www.finishinglinepress.com
also available on amazon.com

Author inquiries and mail orders:
Finishing Line Press
PO Box 1626
Georgetown, Kentucky 40324
USA

Contents

For DK

Akhmatova sees into Kresti
for NHK

Standing on the shore, peering into the
night fog as light permeates the sky, rose
and gold, gold and rose, straining, she can see
nothing, not tower, nor brick, nor window
nor the sun or son still hidden behind
mist, mortar and sad ideology.
The two a.m. spans are closed not a sign
of bridging gaps, but of a time to be
somewhere. Still the uterine pull is keen
as she hopes not to see, but to be seen.

Marie Antoinette

"It's just a phase," they told the worried king
when he asked his doctor about the cuts
on her arms and legs, "a typical thing
in girls to get attention. It is what
they all do—it is no call for alarm
unless they deepen." No matter. She still
has the sun, the wind and rain on her farm,
her children minus one, bread from her mill.
And a noble heart for starving people;
cream puffs and cake are sent with a dimple.

Athena

The reverie broken by staccato shards,
bursts of fire in the east. Golden spindles
weaving blue and yellow, each weft and warp,
alternating rows, until they dwindle
and silence. The sun continues to rise;
bodies covered with hard frost hiss and steam.
A dog wanders lost—his boy now disguised
as a soldier—and in his look, a dream
of a dog in his master's arms, such warmth
in plaid wool, dozing, breathing on the farm.

Lizzie Borden

Don't laugh when you look at me or rather
behind my back I know you do you do
you fuckers, you fuckers, and you fuckers
who took no evidence; of course you lose.
It wasn't forty, wasn't forty-one,
it was quite a few less that did the job,
(like killing pigeons, hack, hack, and you're done)
throw the mess in the furnace, gobbly gob.
And now on the hill, I've no need to roam.
But don't come near me, don't come near my home.

Catherine the Great

The Russian realm is like Izmailovsky—
a glorious facade behind which looms
mud, raw treasure, icons, useful debris—
tortuous paths lain with disease and ruin.
How not to lose one's way? How do you rule
a darkened labyrinth of desert and sky?
By looking up at the stars and so cool
fire with fire—a brilliant ruby set high
enough to see the world to come later:
if women were czars, all would be better.

Elizabeth I

There was never a night that courtiers
stood outside the door, never a morning
billowy sheets were checked by worriers
of the throne. So be it. We are doing
exactly what we want to do between.
Sometimes a carpel, sometimes a stamen,
Raleigh's Gloriana or Spenser's queen,
this one or that—however blows the wind.
But through infidelity, scourge of pox,
there's only one letter—only one box.

Guinevere: through the mists

Yesterday, my old nurse called for nothing;
then she started on about sunset clouds—
it was early morning, the cock had sung
earlier still, and I, listing about,
started a tapestry with cumulus
threads of red and gold, whorled lines that settle
into tangerine/dark gray layered streaks:
joined in thought, do we not test the mettle
of the human coil? A phoenix affects
its doom. If love is love and hate is hate,
who plummets the depths? Who then mates their mate?

Lillian Hellman

When they started calling, we were alert
to names of friends/not friends joining the cult
of fear?/not fear? Free to drink, smoke, and swear
but not free to carry the self-same guilt;
some lesser god, held less accountable—
two women breed tragedy; two men plot.
To live like a man—dash, dash—dash it all.
It is so much more than being a sot.
Goddam the fifth, says the man with the hat,
you wouldn't do well in jail; there are rats.

Jane Doe, found in a dumpster

She knows nothing of knowing. Nothing. Zip.
The blows and slaps fall down her shallow well
of consciousness; the angry voices slip
beneath the silent black surface of hell
she carries with her as she is carried.
Carried, bathed, powdered—squirming to loose the
hold one has on her, all such touch married
to the other. Mother. Is this to be?
Father, will you snuff it out before it
is me? Will I emerge or darkly sit?

Jemima

So, I arrived in the Baltimore docks;
a child sailed from the London workhouses:
an adult was delivered in her smock.
Only nineteen, but what I had seen boasts
not of kindness, but of cold business.
Intended for servitude, I kept watch
over the weakened and crying minors
in the hull; when one died I knew to fetch
the captain. Against the bow, the waves splashed
as a small naked foot slipped past the mast.

Joan of Arc

What was it she said? *What* was it she said?
She talks of assassinations, bullets,
rape, inequities of a punishment
that uses excrement or ice water:
she doesn't want to be stripped and tortured
until blood streams down her legs and falls in
puddles around her feet. Who *is* she? *Who*
is she? She knows too much for her own good.
She works the grey holies until later
than late; what do they *do*? Love or hate her?

Frida Kahlo

There is fierceness that comes through art from pain.
Cheekbone highlights are wads of paint layered
in streaks; our face a canvas crossed with rain—
a flower: bleeding into bloom, but mired
in barbed wire…some painted imbroglio.
Don't look too closely; the pain is the art—
nothing to do at all with the bright show
of hue—broken bones are the other part
of paint showing through. No haughty pretense:
it's in the art of how I carry it.

Lucy

Neither the hunter nor the gatherer,
but one watching infants climb and chatter,
just the one long verb, howl, that is nurture;
our first speech echoing in the laughter
of apish children. A conversation
captured, imprinted in the mire and tar,
silently filed past in orchestration,
reverently observing life so near
to gestation. She tends now, feeling cold.
And unrequited, if the truth be told.

Maria Sibylla Merian
for Polina

Pink toes splay as the hidden hook pierces
a ruby throat below topaz dead eyes
and cockroaches take over the world first
by tentacled pineapple. *Sang-froid*, thy
name is woman among organisms
who struggle. *Mer. surin.* My reference,
(all is nature outside of this prison)
as will be my daughters in due time hence.
Begat and begone are one and the same,
sometimes before breath, sometimes with a name.

Morgan Le Fey

It begins at the end when it is done:
the legend kingdom burnt down by mortal
frailty—chivalry's empty beacon
drained by the denial of human faults.
I captivated all except for one;
your dream of perfection: a living ruse.
In death one is perfect, perfectly done.
Offered immortality who wouldn't choose
the good with the bad, the rave with the sin?
Take my hand. When it is done, it begins.

Rosa Parks

It is a woman's lot to be beaten
and get back up—the strength of the weaker
sex is cool nerves. This was her quickening.
No child, but the birth of a nation. Her
back straight up, her eyes knowing through rimless
glasses—so many times she had followed
the hateful rules, every day, and, yes,
she had worked since seven, to sew and sew,
but that was not the fatigue she could be;
she was tired of arbitrary cruelty.

Salome

It sounds so gross. A head upon a plate.
There'll be people rotting in iron gibbets
along the street—the children even. What
of that? Pretty gross. Not something to fete
like we did Herod's birth (my mother's spouse).
And my lover. I was raised concubine,
to know how to please: use my hips and mouth—
times, they were different; I didn't mind.
You think me wicked for my wayward glance?
Judge her for her acts; judge me by my dance.

Sophie Scholl

"Such a fine, sunny day, I have to go;
but what does my death matter if through us
thousands of people are awakened so
and stirred to action for that which is just."
I feel no pain. The shock of the baton
against my leg was resolute, my limp
barely noticeable beneath my con
of courage to myself; the sun, a glimpse
of Hans, of love, of all I never knew—
but I see you, Beelzebub. I see you.

Mary Shelley

I swear she scares me every night I can't
wrap my head around her brain, her conscious-
ness so far beyond my own raptures scant
words on a page compared to her oceans
of bone dry thought whittled to a graveyard
headstone. My god. I was Humbert, drowning
before youth; a wink and I fell down hard.
But that was nothing; her wit everything…
her mind colossal…wait…let's get one thing straight,
I only edited. There. End of debate.

AKOLOUTE (Sequi me)

Tracing dusty footprints, you can be led
to fornix, to tombs, the circus and bars,
to my lupan, my cell, my earthen bed;
what waits is not secret—see what I are?
I'm not a barmaid, an actor or slave;
I'm not being cursed because I had sinned—
I'm earning my keep in this grisly trade.
For that I am trayf, but come along in.
I'll lead you to places you've never had;
to hell in velvet: it's your bloody as.

Elizabeth L. Hodges' volume of poetry, *Witchery*, was published by MadHat Press in 2016. She is the founding editor of *St. Petersburg Review* and *Springhouse Journal* (springhousejournal.com). Previously she was legal counsel for the New Hampshire court system where she was co-chair of the Vologda/NH Rule of Law Consortium, traveling to Russia a dozen times assisting in establishing an independent judicial branch after perestroika.